THE VALUE OF CURIOSITY

The Story of Christopher Columbus

VALUE COMMUNICATIONS, INC
PUBLISHERS
LA JOLLA, CALIFORNIA

THE VALUE OF CURIOSITY

The Story of
Christopher Columbus

BY SPENCER JOHNSON, M.D.

THE DANBURY PRESS

The Value of Curiosity is part of the ValueTales series.

The Value of Curiosity text copyright © 1977 by Spencer Johnson, M.D. Illustrations copyright © 1977 by Value Communications, Inc.

First Edition
Manufactured in the United States of America
For information write to: ValueTales, P.O. Box 1012
La Jolla, CA 92038

Library of Congress Cataloging in Publication Data

Johnson, Spencer.
    The value of curiosity.

    (ValueTales)
    SUMMARY: Demonstrates the value of curiosity in the life of Christopher Columbus.
    1.   Colombo, Cristoforo—Juvenile literature.
2.   America—Discovery and exploration—Spanish—
Juvenile literature.   3.   Explorers—Spain—Biography—
Juvenile literature.   4.   Curiosity—Juvenile
literature.   [1.   Columbus, Christopher.   2.   Explorers.
3.   Curiosity]   I.   Title.
E111.J68   970.01'5'0924   [B]   [92]   77-11032

ISBN 0-916392-13-9

This tale is about Christopher Columbus,
whose curiosity led to the discovery of the New
World. The story that follows is based on events
in his life. More historical facts about
Christopher Columbus can be found on page 63.

Once upon a time...

long ago—so long ago that most people still thought the world was flat—there lived a little boy named Christopher Columbus.

Little Christopher liked to stand at the window of his father's weaving shop and look out at the port city of Genoa, Italy.

What do you suppose Christopher saw when he looked out? And what do you suppose he thought about?

Why, he saw the ships in the harbor. And he thought about how they sailed off to faraway places. Of course, the ships didn't sail as far then as they do now. In those days, the sailors did not like to lose sight of land.

One day, Christopher and his little brothers went down to the wharf to get a closer look at the ships. "You know," said one of Christopher's brothers, "if you sail too far from shore, you'll end up in the Sea of Darkness, where no stars ever shine."

8

"And monsters hide out there in the dark," said the other little brother. "There's an ocean of seaweed that catches ships and holds them so that they never get away!"

"I wonder if all that's really true," said Christopher.

Just then, two sailors came strolling along the dock.

"Excuse me!" called Christopher to the men. "Can you tell us if the stories about the Sea of Darkness are true? And is there really an ocean of seaweed that catches ships and holds them forever? Are there monsters out there? If ships sail too far out, can they fall off the edge of the world?"

One of the sailors chuckled. "We can have some fun with these youngsters!" he whispered to his friend.

The sailor made a scary face. "It's all true," he said. "There are islands in the Sea of Darkness that appear and disappear like magic. You can hear bells ringing under the sea, and see ghostly horses race over the waves. The terrible seaweed stretches for miles, waiting to snare unwary ships. It's frightening out there, little mates—very frightening indeed!"

Christopher agreed this was frightening. Just the same, he decided that when he grew up he'd go to sea and find out for himself what was true and what wasn't.

11

"I'll be a ship's captain," he said. And as soon as he was old enough, he went to sea as a cabin boy. That was the way a seafarer began in those days. He worked hard. He swept out the cabins and made the beds and brought the captain his meals. He was very happy to be on a ship, going to sea.

He was standing at the rail one day, looking out at the water, when a seagull swooped down and landed almost at his elbow.

"Hi, Chris," said the bird. "My name's See. See Gull. I've been watching you, and you look as if you're thinking some very important thoughts. I'm curious. Just what are you thinking about?"

Christopher blinked. "I didn't know that seagulls talked," said he. But then he laughed out loud. Of course seagulls didn't talk. This particular seagull was just a make-believe friend. It was Christopher himself, having fun, pretending that he could chat with a bird.

"Well, Mr. Gull," said Christopher, "I was really . . ."

"You can call me See," interrupted the bird. "That's what they named me because I like to fly around and see things. You understand how it is. I'm curious!"

"Curious?" said Christopher. "I don't know what that word means, but . . ."

"It means I have lots of curiosity," said the bird. "I wonder about things, and I try to find out about them."

"Well," said Christopher, "I guess I have a lot of curiosity myself. I was just wondering about what's on the other side of the ocean."

"That's great!" said See. "When will you try to find out?"

"Just as soon as I can," answered Christopher.

And sure enough, as he grew older, Christopher became more and more curious about what was on the far side of the ocean. He kept sailing on ships. He kept studying maps and charts, too. At last he became a map-maker himself. See Gull, his imaginary friend, was pleased about this.

"I'm finding out more about the world all the time," said Christopher, "and that makes me feel very good!"

"Me, too!" laughed See Gull.

One day Christopher read a book about Marco Polo and his journey to the eastern lands called the Indies. It told about emperors who lived in beautiful palaces filled with spices and gold and silk. "I want to go to the Indies like Marco Polo," thought Christopher. "I want to see all those wonderful things with my own eyes."

Soon after this, Christopher was walking on the beach. To his surprise he found an unusual piece of carved wood and some pieces of a strange plant. They had been washed up by the waves. Christopher picked up the wood. "How odd," he said. "I've never seen anything like this before."

"Neither have I," said See Gull, "and I fly to lots of places and see many things."

Christopher put the wood in his pocket, and he picked up the pieces of the plant. "Come on, See," he said. "We'll try to find out about these things."

But even the wisest man in the land couldn't tell Christopher anything about the wood and the plant. "I'm sorry," said the wise man, "but I have no idea what these are, or where they came from."

Now Christopher was filled with curiosity. "They had to come from somewhere," he said. He went off by himself to think about it.

After a while, he thought he knew where they came from.

Do you know?

"They came from the other side of the ocean!" he exclaimed. "The book about Marco Polo's travels is a true story. He really did see the land called the Indies, and it was filled with strange things and odd plants and trees. Suppose the wisest navigators are right. Suppose the world is really round, like an apple!"

"But almost everybody says it's flat," See Gull declared.

"What if they are wrong?" asked Christopher. "What if the world *is* round? Why couldn't the piece of wood and the plant float here from the other side of the ocean? And if they floated here, why couldn't we go there? We could sail west, and come all the way around to the same place Marco Polo found when he traveled east by land!"

"Terrific idea!" cried See Gull. But then the bird looked a bit worried. "But what about the Sea of Darkness?" he said. "Doesn't it scare you?"

"Of course it does," admitted Christopher. "But I'm curious. And if I want to find the truth, I have to take some chances!"

"Well, if you must, you must," said See Gull. "But if you're going to sail to the far side of the ocean, you'll need money for ships and supplies."

"Only kings and queens have that much money," said Christopher, and he set out to see the rulers of all the nearby countries.

No one was curious enough to help him. But then Columbus met Queen Isabella and King Ferdinand of Spain. "It would be wonderful to have a sea route to the Indies," they said. "We might help you. But we'll have to think about it for a while."

Christopher Columbus waited while Isabella and Ferdinand thought it over. He waited and waited and waited. He waited for six years!

Of course he kept studying and working so that he'd be ready when the chance came. But every now and then he'd get discouraged. "Don't they have any curiosity?" he asked himself. "Don't they want to find out what lies on the other side of the ocean?"

Christopher had almost given up hope when word came at last. Queen Isabella was now very, very curious about the far side of the ocean. She was giving Columbus three ships—the Nina, the Pinta, and the Santa Maria. And she was giving him the supplies he would need for his voyage.

At first Columbus was delighted. But then he found that getting the ships was the easiest part. What do you think was going to be harder?

Getting the sailors to go on the voyage was going to be harder. In fact, it was going to be almost impossible. Columbus explained about the sea route to the Indies. He coaxed and he pleaded. But were the sailors in a hurry to sign up for this voyage to the other side of the ocean?

No! They most certainly were not!

"We'll never reach the Indies!" warned one man.

"There are monsters beyond the Sea of Darkness," said another.

"They're huge monsters who can swallow whole ships!" moaned a third sailor.

"Even if the monsters don't get us, we're doomed if we go too far," said a fourth man. "Remember that the world is flat. If we sail off the edge, we'll be lost forever."

Then Columbus asked a very good question. "How could anyone know about monsters, or about the edge of the world, if no one had ever sailed there before?"

"Say, that's right!" shouted a seaman. "If we want to know what's true, we have to go and find out for ourselves. I've gotten to wondering, and I'm too curious to stay home. I'll make the voyage!"

"Good for you!" said Columbus. "There's something else you might like to know. Queen Isabella is offering a rich reward to all who sail with me."

And so the men agreed to go, and Columbus had his crew.

On August 3, 1492, the three ships sailed out of the Spanish harbor of Palos. Columbus was full of hope. He even carried with him letters from King Ferdinand and Queen Isabella to the emperors of the Indies.

The ships sailed west. On and on they went until the land disappeared behind them and the sea stretched around them in all directions. A silence had come over the men. They now knew that no ship had ever before come so far. Then, suddenly, a man cried out in fright!

"An ocean of seaweed!" he shouted. "We're sailing right into it!"

"It will catch us!" cried a second man. "We'll never get away!"

It seemed true. There was seaweed on the surface of the ocean for as far as the eye could see. The sailors were sure that the seaweed had roots going all the way down to the bottom of the sea. They thought that the ships would get tangled in the weed. They feared that they would never escape.

"Don't worry," said Christopher. "Look at that seaweed! It's not thick. It's just floating on top of the water. We can sail right through it."

And sure enough, the ships did sail through! As they went, Columbus noticed something interesting. He scooped up a handful of the weed and showed it to the sailors.

What do you think they saw?

"See the little crab on the seaweed?" said Columbus. "How can land be far away when such creatures are crawling around here? Have faith. We must be nearing the Indies."

The men felt better then. They even began to be curious. They wondered what it would be like when they reached the Indies. But when Columbus put the crab back on the seaweed and went off by himself, his face was serious and sober.

"I hope that little crab *is* a land creature," Christopher said to See. "We've been at sea so long. Sometimes even I begin to wonder if we'll ever see land again."

"When you do something that you've never done before, it's bound to be scary," said See. "But it's a good thing we have brave, curious people like you, Christopher, or we'd never find out *anything*!"

Christopher would have liked to talk with See a little longer, but he suddenly heard a loud noise. The deck tilted under his feet.

A fierce wind had come up without any warning. It roared around the ships and tossed the sailors to the decks. It caught See and slammed the poor bird against a mast.

Christopher caught See and held him fast. "Are you all right?" he shouted.

"I'm afraid my wing is broken!" squawked See.

The sailors cowered down and clutched at ropes and railings as the wind shrieked and howled like an angry monster. Then, almost as suddenly as it had started, the wind stopped. The raging sea became as calm as a pond.

The sailors were quiet. They were frightened. Do you know why no wind at all would frighten the sailors just as much as a heavy gale?

That's right. Without any wind in the sails, the ship was becalmed. It wouldn't move at all.

The sailors began to mutter among themselves.

"We'll never get home," said one man. "We'll stay here in the middle of the ocean until we all die."

"I wish Columbus would fall overboard," said another.

"Don't say that!" cried a third man. "Without Columbus to navigate, we might never find our way home!"

So the men watched the dolphins play near the ship, and they waited anxiously.

Columbus waited, too. And of course, since See was really just Christopher's own thoughts, See was with him in his cabin.

"How long will we be becalmed in these unknown seas?" Christopher wondered aloud.

"There's no way to tell," said See. "That's what makes it so scary."

Finally, after many days, a gentle wind began to blow. They were traveling on again, and little waves were slapping against the hull of the ship. The men on deck could laugh again, and wonder what they would find when they reached the Indies. Even See's wing felt better. He thought he would be able to fly again very soon.

And so they sailed at a good speed for many days. Then, at last, they heard the sound they had been waiting for. A cannon boomed from one of the ships. "Land!" shouted a sailor. "I see land!"

But when Christopher and the other men looked out across the water, they saw no land. The sailor had been mistaken. There was no safe harbor where they could anchor, and no place to rest. There was only water—miles and miles of water.

They sailed on. There was nothing else they could do. But now the crew didn't feel frightened. They didn't feel curious, either. How do you suppose they felt?

They felt angry!

"We want to go home!" they shouted to Columbus. "If you don't turn the ships around, we will!"

"That's mutiny!" thought See.

"You'll go to prison if you do that!" shouted Columbus.

"We don't care!" cried the men.

40

Desperate, Columbus tried to awaken the sailors' curiosity. "Don't you want to find out what's on the other side of the ocean?" he asked. "Don't you want to go home and tell your children and grandchildren that you were the first ones to sail to the Indies?"

"If we don't turn back, we may never see our children and grandchildren again," said the men.

"Let's sail for three more days," said Columbus. "If we don't sight land by then, we'll turn back."

The men grumbled and muttered, but they agreed to sail on.

"We must be getting near the place where the world ends," said one man. He listened for the thunder of the waterfall that would surely take place when the ocean poured over the edge of the world. He began to tremble. "I don't hear anything yet," he said hopefully.

"Yes, but I don't *see* any land either. All I see is water. If there *is* land ahead, I wonder what it will be like. Will it be the Indies? Will there be golden palaces?"

"I don't think there is any land," said a third man. "We'll have to turn back."

Suddenly the men heard a noise high above them. It was a soft, hurrying, flapping noise.

What do you suppose it was?

"Birds!" shouted a happy sailor. "It's a flock of birds!"

"At last!" cried See. "That means there's land! Land nearby!"

The sailors cheered, for of course See was right.
Birds couldn't fly endlessly over an ocean. They
needed a place to land and rest their wings. At last
they were close to land.

So the ships changed course, and they followed the birds.

And now that they were so very close to safety, the men began to wonder. What kind of place was it that they were coming to?

Well, they soon knew that it was a place where there were trees and bushes and lots of green growing things, for they saw twigs and leaves and fresh little red berries floating in the water.

"It won't be long now," they said eagerly.

Night fell, but no one thought of sleeping. They all watched. Then suddenly one of the men saw something—a dark mass rising from the water, very black and huge. Was it a monster?

The cannon boomed, and the crew came running, eager to see.

"Land!" they shouted. "Land ahead!"

There it was at last! A small island lay just before
them, rising up out of the water.

The flags were raised on all three ships. The cannon
boomed again—so loudly that the sleepy moon
seemed to stir a bit. Perhaps it looked down and
asked what these men were doing there, and why
they were making so much noise.

"It's beautiful, isn't it?" Columbus said to See. "I was beginning to be afraid we'd never get here. I wonder what it's like?"

Columbus wasn't the only one who was curious. The entire crew had crowded against the railings to look at the island. They could hardly wait until morning.

At dawn, Columbus and some of his men climbed into a small boat. See perched on the prow, and they rowed toward the shore.

Columbus reached inside his coat to make sure that his important letters were safe. They were the letters of greeting that Queen Isabella had given him. He was to present them to the Emperor of India and the Emperor of China.

Christopher Columbus was in for a surprise.

There wasn't a single emperor waiting on the beach. In fact, there was no one waiting on the beach. Columbus saw only white sand and blue sky—and some bushes.

"These are the same sort of plants that we saw washed up on the shore at home," Columbus said to See. "I was right. They did come from the far side of the ocean."

Just then the bushes moved. Someone was hiding there!

51

"Why, these must be Indians," said Columbus, when some people with red-brown skin came out to greet him.

Columbus had made a very natural mistake. He thought he had landed in the Indies. So, even though these people didn't look a bit like the yellow-skinned people Marco Polo had described, he called them Indians.

Now of course you know where Columbus actually had landed! Don't you?

That's right! He was in America!

He was on the island of San Salvador, off the coast of America.

The islanders were very friendly. They didn't seem to mind being called Indians, and they showed their island to Columbus. They showed him some neighboring islands, too. They couldn't show him any emperors or great cities or gold. They didn't have any.

"I'm a little disappointed," said Columbus to See.

See was quite well by now, and no longer had a bandage on his wing. He laughed a loud seagull laugh. "When you're curious and you go looking for answers, you may not find the ones you expect," he said. "That's part of the excitement."

"I hope Queen Isabella will be excited," said Columbus. "And I hope she'll like what we've found."

So, after looking around for several months, Columbus and his crew set sail for home. They had lots of interesting things to show to the Queen—trees and plants. Even some of the Indians went back with Columbus. They were curious, too, and wanted to see what was on the other side of the ocean.

The voyage back to Spain was stormy, but at last they arrived home with their strange cargoes.

"We did it!" said the sailors proudly. "We didn't turn back! We were with Columbus, and we found a new land!"

The sailors hurried home to tell their families that they hadn't fallen off the edge of the world. And that they hadn't been attacked by monsters. Christopher Columbus immediately went to see the Queen.

"I have been to the other side of the ocean," he told Queen Isabella. "I have found a strange new land, and I have brought back many interesting things for you."

Then Columbus showed the Queen's advisors a map he had made. It was like no other map ever made before. It showed the ocean, and the islands he had seen on the far side.

"I know that this is a true map," said Columbus. "I made it only after I had been to these islands myself. I'm sure, though, that there are other places where no one has ever been. Who will draw the maps of these other places? Who has enough curiosity to go and find out about them?"

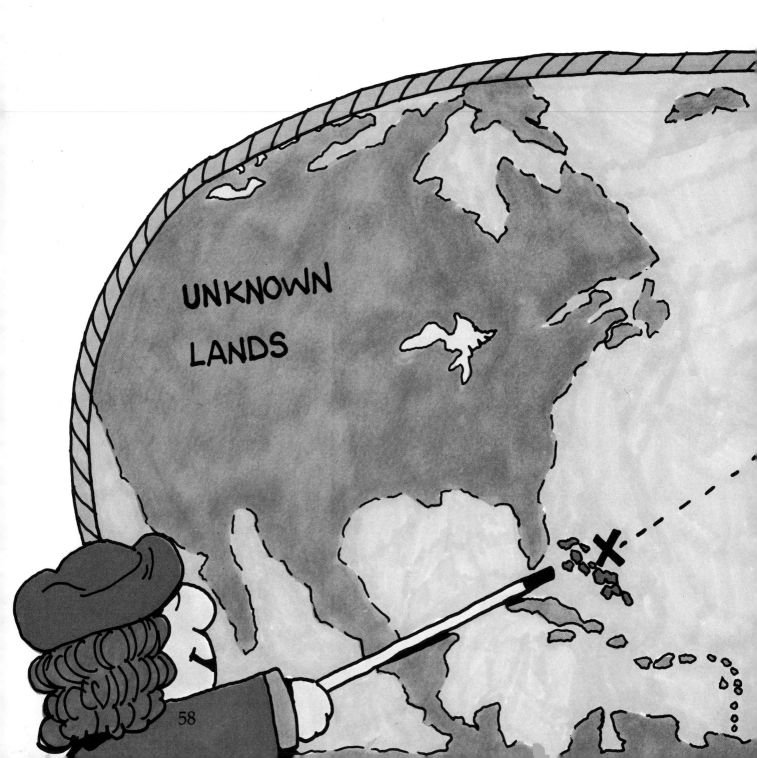

"I am not a sailor," said the Queen, "but I am full of curiosity. I will help you. I'll see to it that you can sail to the New World you have found just as often as you wish."

Even then, Columbus did not know what a truly great discovery he had made. Until his voyage, no one in Europe had even suspected that there were two huge continents—North America and South America—on the other side of the ocean.

Later, with the help of the wise Queen, Christopher sailed back to America three more times. He continued to be curious. He continued trying to learn new things. Even when he didn't find anything, he knew it was fun just to look.

Because Christopher was curious, he opened the way for later explorations. And because he was curious, we will never forget Christopher Columbus.

Now you may wonder about the value of curiosity in your own life. Is there something you would like to learn more about?

Not everyone has to be curious, of course. It's up to you. But if you are curious you may find out some wonderful things.

Whatever you decide to do, let's hope it is something that will make you happier.

Just like our curious friend, Christopher Columbus.

The End

Christopher Columbus was born sometime between August 25 and October 31, 1451 in the seaport city of Genoa, Italy. His father was a woolweaver.

At the age of fourteen, Columbus began a seafaring career. Between voyages to the then known parts of the world, Columbus kept busy with the making and selling of charts and maps.

An experienced seafarer and a student of nautical science, it is not surprising that Columbus concluded that he could reach the rich continent of Asia by sailing West. Columbus was fascinated by Marco Polo's account of his travels to Asia in 1275, over two hundred years before Columbus' first voyage to the New World.

Columbus might not have undertaken his historic voyage except for a single off chance event. While walking near his home on the Portuguese island of Madeira, he discovered strange plants and pieces of wood washed up on the beach. Columbus concluded that these foreign objects must have drifted across the ocean from unknown lands.

While other mariners were struggling to reach Asia by sailing east around the tip of Africa, Columbus believed that a western route was infinitely shorter. By his calculations the route was only 2,400 miles. He was wrong. Little did Columbus know that not less than 10,000 nautical miles lay between Western Europe and Asia.

Columbus first discussed his plan with King John the Second of Portugal in 1484. But after months of waiting he was refused any help. He then traveled to Spain. But Queen Isabella thought Columbus' price too high. Instead of one ship, he wanted three. And if he reached the Indies he asked for a title, a coat of arms and one-tenth of all the profits brought to Spain. Columbus waited six years.
Finally discouraged, Columbus set out to seek the support of the French King. But a powerful official of the Spanish court, Luis de Santangel, advised Isabella to change her mind. Columbus was four miles out of town when the Queen's courier caught up with him.

Even after the Queen had granted Columbus three ships, it was difficult to get a crew to sail with him. Evidence of the unpopularity of the expedition is shown by a royal decree of April 30,

CHRISTOPHER COLUMBUS
1451–1506

1492 ordering the suspension of judicial proceedings against criminals, provided they sailed with Columbus. It was this document that probably started the myth that Columbus' crew consisted entirely of prisoners. In fact, only four men took advantage of this decree. When a respected shipper, Martin Alonso Pinzon, agreed to sail on the Pinta, he encouraged the rest of the sailors to sign on for the historic voyage.

On August 3, 1492 Columbus sailed from the port of Palos in Andalusia, Spain. After a month on open sea, it was clear that the task was a larger one than they had imagined. The men complained and threatened to turn back whether Columbus ordered it or not.

Finally on October 12, 1492, at 2 a.m., seventy-one days after leaving Spain, a sailor on the Pinta, Rodrigo de Triana shouted "Tierra! Tierra!" Land! Land! The island of San Salvador, three hundred seventy-five miles southeast of the coast of Florida, had been sighted. Columbus spent more than three months in the Caribbean before returning to Spain.

Columbus was to make three more voyages from Spain to look in vain for the Indies. He discovered many of the Caribbean Islands as well as South America and Central America. Columbus never landed on the mainland of North America. But he had paved the way for other explorers and had forever changed the course of history.

Other Titles in the ValueTale Series